Creative Problem Solving

90 Minute Guides

Michelle N. Halsey

Silver City Publications & Training, L.L.C.
P.O. Box 1914
Nampa, ID 83653
https://www.silvercitypublications.com/shop/

ISBN-10: 1-64004-014-5
ISBN-13: 978-1-64004-014-4

Contents

Chapter 1 – Getting Started

Welcome to the Creative Problem Solving workshop. In the past few decades, psychologists and business people alike have discovered that successful problem solvers tend to use the same type of process to identify and implement the solutions to their problems. This process works for any kind of problem, large or small.

This workshop will give participants an overview of the entire creative problem solving process, as well as key problem solving tools that they can use every day.

Research has consistently demonstrated that when clear goals are associated with learning that the learning occurs more easily and rapidly. With that in mind, let's review our goals for today.

By the end of this tutorial, you will be able to:

• Understand problems and the creative problem solving process

• Identify types of information to gather and key questions to ask in problem solving

• Identify the importance of defining a problem correctly

• Identify and use four different problem definition tools

• Write concrete problem statements

• Use basic brainstorming tools to generate ideas for solutions

• Use idea generating tools, such as affinity diagrams, word chaining, the box method, the six thinking hats, and the blink method

• Evaluate potential solutions against criteria, including cost/benefit analysis and group voting

• Perform a final analysis to select a solution

• Understand the roles that fact and intuition play in selecting a solution

- Understand the need to refine the shortlist and re-refine it

- Understand how to identify the tasks and resources necessary to implement solutions

- Evaluate and adapt solutions to reality

- Follow up with solution implementation to celebrate successes and identify improvements

Think of a problem that you need to solve. It could be a work problem, like a difficult customer problem, or a home problem, like dealing with a teenage that stays out too late.

Take a few moments to write the basic information about your problem here.

Chapter 2 – The Problem Solving Method

To begin, let's look at the creative problem solving process. In this chapter, we will define "problem" and other situations that lend themselves to the creative problem solving process. We will introduce the concept of solving problems using a creative process. The approach we use in this course includes six steps, which are also introduced in this chapter.

What is a Problem?

The Random House Unabridged Dictionary includes several definitions for the word "problem." The definitions that we are most concerned with while learning about the creative problem solving process are:

- "any question or matter involving doubt, uncertainty, or difficulty," and

- "a question proposed for solution or discussion."

A problem can be defined as a scenario in which the current situation does not match the desired situation, or anytime actual performance does not match expectations. Other labels for a problem include challenges or opportunities, or any situation or circumstance for which there is room for improvement.

What is Creative Problem Solving?

Creative problem solving has evolved since its inception in the 1950s. However, it is always a structured approach to finding and implementing solutions.

The creative problem solving process involves creativity. The problem solvers come up with solutions that are innovative, rather than obtaining help to learn the answers or implementing standard procedures.

The creative problem solving process is at work anytime you identify solutions that have value or that somehow improve a situation for someone.

What are the Steps in the Creative Solving Process?

The Creative Problem Solving Process uses six major steps to implement solutions to almost any kind of problem. The steps are:

1. Information Gathering, or understanding more about the problem before proceeding

2. Problem Definition, or making sure you understand the correct problem before proceeding

3. Generating Possible Solutions using various tools

4. Analyzing Possible Solutions, or determining the effectiveness of possible solutions before proceeding

5. Selecting the Best Solution(s)

6. Planning the Next Course of Action (Next Steps), or implementing the solution(s)

Case Study

Carl and Nathan were exhausted after spending their evening at work, trying to figure out how to solve the logistic problem of how many pallets of flour should go to each grocery store. They were ready to give up, until Carl suggested they use the Creative Problem Solving Process to discover the best solutions and next course of action. Using the six steps, Nathan and Carl wrote down and defined the problem, before discovering suitable solutions and selecting the best one. They were glad to get off work, once they had planned their next course of action, and relieved that the problem had finally been solved, and that the grocery stores would receive the correct amounts of flour.

Chapter 3 – Information Gathering

The first step in the creative problem solving process is to gather information about the problem. In order to effectively solve the correct problem, you need to know as much about it as possible. In this chapter, we will explore different types of information, key questions, and different methods used to gather information.

Understanding Types of Information

There are many different types of information. The following list includes information you will need to consider when beginning the creative problem solving process:

- Fact

- Opinion

- Opinionated Fact

- Concept

- Assumption

- Procedure

- Process

- Principle

Facts are small pieces of well-known data. Facts are based on objective details and experience. Opinions are also based on observation and experience, but they are subjective and can be self-serving. When a fact and opinion are presented together, it is an opinionated fact, which may try to indicate the significance of a fact, suggest generalization, or attach value to it. Opinionated facts are often meant to sway the listener to a particular point of view using the factual data.

Concepts are general ideas or categories of items or ideas that share common features. Concepts are important pieces of information to help make connections or to develop theories or hypotheses.

Assumptions are a type of concept or hypothesis in which something is taken for granted.

Procedures are a type of information that tells how to do something with specific steps. Processes are slightly different, describing continuous actions or operations to explain how something works or operates. Principles are accepted rules or fundamental laws or doctrines, often describing actions or conduct.

Identifying Key Questions

When tackling a new problem, it is important to talk to anyone who might be familiar with the problem. You can gather a great deal of information by asking questions of different people who might be affected by or know about the problem. Remember to ask people with years of experience in the organization, and lower-level employees. Sometimes their insights can provide valuable information about a problem.

What questions should you ask? The key questions will be different for every situation. Questions that begin with the following are always a good starting point:

- Who?

- What?

- Which?

- Where?

- When?

- Why?

- How?

Here are some examples of more specific questions:

- Who initially defined the problem?

- What is the desired state?

- What extent is the roof being damaged?

- Where is the water coming from?

- When did the employee finish his training?

- How can we increase our market share?

- Which equipment is working?

One important source of information on a problem is to ask if it has been solved before. Find out if anyone in your company or network has had the same problem. This can generate great information about the problem and potential solutions.

Methods of Gathering Information

When gathering information about a problem, there are several different methods you can use. No one method is better than another. The method depends on the problem and other circumstances. Here are some of the ways you can collect information about a problem:

- Conduct interviews.

- Identify and study statistics.

- Send questionnaires out to employees, customers, or other people concerned with the problem.

- Conduct technical experiments.

- Observe the procedures or processes in question first hand.

- Create focus groups to discuss the problem.

Case Study

Julia was surrounded by mounds of papers, and couldn't figure out how to approach the problem of organizing them into files for the next day's meeting. She decided to approach Leonard, her assistant, and asked if he could help her. He suggested they use the Identifying

Key Questions to gather information about the problem and figure out what the desired state for the filing would be. Julia and Leonard brainstormed the answers to these key questions, and were happy when they could figure out the best methods of organizing the paperwork and relieving that excess pressure and workload on Julia's desk.

Chapter 4 — Problem Definition

The next step in the creative problem solving process is to identify the problem. This chapter will explore why problem solvers need to clearly define the problem. It also introduces several tools to use when defining a problem and writing a problem statement.

Defining the Problem

When a problem comes to light, it may not be clear exactly what the problem is. You must understand the problem before you spend time or money implementing a solution.

It is important to take care in defining the problem. The way that you define your problem influences the solution or solutions that are available. Problems often can be defined in many different ways. You must address the true problem when continuing the creative problem solving process in order to achieve a successful solution. You may come up with a terrific solution, but if it is a solution to the wrong problem, it will not be a success.

In some cases, taking action to address a problem before adequately identifying the problem is worse than doing nothing. It can be a difficult task to sort out the symptoms of the problem from the problem itself. However, it is important to identify the underlying problem in order to generate the right solutions. Problem solvers can go down the wrong path with possible solutions if they do not understand the true problem. These possible solutions often only treat the symptoms of the problem, and not the real problem itself.

Four tools to use in defining the problem are:

- Determining where the problem originated

- Defining the present state and the desired state

- Stating and restating the problem

- Analyzing the problem

You may not use all of these tools to help define a problem. Different tools lend themselves to some kinds of problems better than other kinds.

Determining Where the Problem Originated

Successful problem solvers get to the root of the problem by interviewing or questioning anyone who might know something useful about the problem. Ask questions about the problem, including questions that:

- Clarify the situation

- Challenge assumptions about the problem

- Determine possible reasons and evidence

- Explore different perspectives concerning the problem

- Ask more about the original question

If you did not define the problem, find out who did. Think about that person's motivations. Challenge their assumptions to dig deeper into the problem.

Defining the Present State and the Desired State

When using this tool, you write a statement of the situation as it currently exists. Then you write a statement of what you would like the situation to look like. The desired state should include concrete details and should not contain any information about possible causes or solutions. Refine the descriptions for each state until the concerns and needs identified in the present state are addressed in the desired state.

Stating and Restating the Problem

The problem statement and restatement technique also helps evolve the understanding of the problem. First write a statement of the problem, no matter how vague. Then use various triggers to help identify the true problem. The triggers are:

- Place emphasis on different words in the statement and ask questions about each emphasis.

- Replace one word in the statement with a substitute that explicitly defines the word to reframe the problem.

- Rephrase the statement with positives instead of negatives or negatives instead of positives to obtain an opposite problem.

- Add or change words that indicate quantity or time, such as always, never, sometimes, every, none or some.

- Identify any persuasive or opinionated words in the statement. Replace or eliminate them.

- Try drawing a picture of the problem or writing the problem as an equation.

Analyzing the Problem

When the cause of the problem is not known, such as in troubleshooting operations, you can look at the what, where, who, and extent of the problem to help define it.

What? - "What" questions help to identify the problem. Use "what" questions both to identify what the problem is, as well as what the problem is not. "What" questions can also help identify a possible cause.

Where? - "Where" questions help to locate the problem. Use "where" questions to distinguish the difference between locations where the problem exists and where it does not exist.

When? - "When" questions help discover the timing of the problem. Use "when" questions to distinguish the difference between when the problem occurs and when it does not, or when the problem was first observed and when it was last observed.

Extent? – Questions that explore the magnitude of the problem include:

- How far vs. how localized?

- How many units are affected vs. how many units are not affected?

- How much of something is affected vs. how much is not affected?

Examining the distinctions between what, where, when, and to what extent the problem **is** and what, where, when and to what extent it **is not** can lead to helpful insights about the problem. Remember to sharpen the statements as the problem becomes clearer.

Writing the Problem Statement

Writing an accurate problem statement can help accurately represent the problem. This helps clarify unclear problems. The problem statement may evolve through the use of the four problem definition tools and any additional information gathered about the problem. As the statement becomes more refined, the types and effectiveness of potential solutions are improved.

The problem statement should:

- Include specific details about the problem, including who, what, when, where, and how

- Address the scope of the problem to identify boundaries of what you can reasonably solve

The problem statement should not include:

- Any mention of possible causes

- Any potential solutions

A detailed, clear, and concise problem statement will provide clear-cut goals for focus and direction for coming up with solutions.

Case Study

Cassidy and Dan were stuck negotiating prices for a new product they'd introduced. The toy cost a certain amount to manufacture, but the price was too high to successfully market and mass produce, whilst making a profit. Dan suggested they use the Stating and Restating method to state and restate the problem, and discuss the positives of the situation and how to best approach solving it. Cassidy and Dan brainstormed and restated their issues with funding as well as the cost of producing their toy and finally came to a solution, which would help them produce and sell the toy at a profit. Cassidy and Dan were happy to implement this idea and see their business prosper in the long run.

Chapter 5 – Preparing for Brainstorming

Before we learn ways to generate solutions in the problem solving process, we will prepare the way for creativity. This chapter introduces common mental blocks to productive brainstorming, as well as techniques for dealing with the mental blocks. It also presents some ideas for stimulating creativity.

Identifying Mental Blocks

Brainstorming can help you arrive at a solution to the problem, even for problems that seem unsolvable or that seem to only have inadequate solutions. However, before beginning a successful brainstorming session to generate ideas, you must remove any mental blocks. Mental blocks can eliminate great solutions before they are thoroughly examined as possibilities or springboards to other possible solutions.

There are many types of mental blocks. Most blocks to problem-solving fit into the following categories.

- **Emotions**: Emotional blocks can include anything from a fear of risk taking to a tendency to judge or approach the problem with a negative attitude.

- **Distractions**: Too much information, irrelevant information, or environmental distractions can prevent a productive brainstorming session.

- **Assumptions**: If problem solvers assume there is only one correct solution, they will be unable to generate additional ideas. Assumptions also become mental blocks from stereotypes or perceived boundaries where none exist.

- **Culture**: Culture defines the way we live and limits the ideas we may generate or consider. However, not every culture is the same. Sometimes the cultural blocks are unnecessary, and sometimes we do not consider cultural limitations when we should.

- **Communication difficulties:** If we cannot communicate our ideas in some way – speaking, writing, or pictures – these communication difficulties can block our progress in generating ideas.

Removing Mental Blocks

So what do you do when you identify a mental block? Carol Goman has identified several structured techniques for blockbusting.

The first technique is an attitude adjustment. To remove blocks arising from a negative attitude, list the positive aspects or possible outcomes of the problem. Remember that problems are also opportunities for improvement.

The next technique deals with risk taking. To remove emotional blocks arising from a fear of failure, define the risk, then indicate why it is important. Define what the worst possible outcome might be and what options there are in that scenario. Think about how to deal with that possible failure.

The next technique encourages you to break the rules. Some rules are important, but when rules create an unnecessary imaginary boundary, they must be disregarded so that problem solvers can come up with innovative solutions.

The fourth technique is to allow imagination, feelings, and a sense of humor to overcome a reliance on logic and a need to conduct problem solving in a step-by-step manner.

The fifth technique involves encouraging your creativity. We'll look at that in more detail in the next topic.

Stimulating Creativity

The creative problem solving process requires creativity. However, many people feel that they are not creative. This is the sign of a mental block at work. Everyone can tap into creative resources in their brains. Sometimes, it just takes a little extra prodding.

Creativity is not something to be turned on and off when needed. The potential for creativity is always there. We just need to learn how to access it.

Here are some tips for creating a creative mental space to encourage productive brainstorming sessions.

- Go outside for a few minutes, especially for a nature walk or bike ride. Exercising and getting sunshine even for just a few minutes are sure ways to redirect your brain to a more creative outlook.

- Change your perspective. Work on the floor or go to the park for you brainstorming session.

- Breathe deeply. Especially when stressed, we tend to become shallow breathers. Fill your entire lungs with air to get some extra oxygen to your brain. Practice deep breathing for 5 to 15 minutes for not only more creativity, but for a great burst of energy.

- Meditate. Focus intently on a candle flame or find another way to quiet your mind of all of your responsibilities and distractions. For a group, try guided meditation.

- Write in a journal. Write for 15-20 minutes in a spare notebook or plain paper. It does not have to be about the specific problem you need to solve, but you may discover some mental blocks if you do write about the problem. Dump all of your mental clutter on to one to three pages that no one will ever see (unless you want them to). Then let the pages and their recorded thoughts go, even if just in your mind.

Once you get your creative juices flowing, keep them going by trying the following ideas everyday:

- Carry a small notebook or jot ideas in your PDA. Be prepared for ideas whenever they come. Ideas often come as you are drifting off to sleep or as you are waking.

- Stretch your boundaries by posing new questions to yourself, learning things outside your specialty, or breaking up set patterns of doing things.

- Be receptive to new, fragile ideas that may still need time to develop.

- Be observant of details, including self-details.

- Find a creative hobby, including working puzzles and playing games.

Case Study

Hercules, Bill and Richard were brainstorming new ideas for a business venture regarding real estate. They were surrounded by empty sheets of paper and were close to fighting with each other, until Bill suggested they use the method of Identifying Mental Blocks. Richard and Hercules agreed, and they set out defining their blocks, including those emotional and block of distraction, as well as the cultural blocks they were experiencing with each other. Together, they put aside their assumptions, communicated their difficulties and worked towards a better brainstorming session because of this. All three men were pleased when they managed to brainstorm an effective idea for the future of their joint venture.

Brainstorm Activity

Who do you ask about this problem? What questions do you ask to find out where this problem came from?

Create a present state statement and a desired state statement. Refine the statements until the desired state statement clearly addresses the needs or issues identified in the present state statement.

Now start with a general statement of the problem and refine it until you reach a concrete problem statement.

Analyze the problem using the following chart.

	THE PROBLEM IS...	THE PROBLEM IS NOT...
WHAT		

WHEN		
WHERE		
EXTENT		

Write the final problem statement.

Chapter 6 – Generating Solutions

Generating possibilities for solutions to the defined problem comes next in the process. It is important to generate as many solutions as possible before analyzing the solutions or trying to implement them. There are many different methods for generating solutions. This chapter begins with some ground rules for brainstorming sessions. Then it presents several idea-generating techniques, including free-association style brainstorming, brain-writing, mind mapping, and Duncker Diagrams.

Brainstorming Basics

In order to come up with a good idea, you must come up with many ideas. The first rule of brainstorming is to come up with as many ideas as you possibly can.

Some of the ideas will not be good. If you start analyzing the ideas while you are generating them, the creative process will quickly come to a halt, and you may miss out on some great ideas. Therefore, the second rule for brainstorming sessions is to defer judgment.

Allow creativity and imagination to take over in this phase of the process. The next rule for brainstorming is to come up with the wildest, most imaginative solutions to your problem that you can. Often we might not consider a solution because of assumptions or associational constraints. However, sometimes those solutions, even if you do not end up implementing them, can lead you to a successful solution. So along with deferring judgment, allow those ideas that might be considered crazy to flow. One of those crazy ideas might just contain the seeds of the perfect solution.

Finally, use early ideas as springboards to other ideas. This is called "piggybacking" and is the next rule for brainstorming.

Basic Brainstorming is a free-association session of coming up with ideas. Use the other group member's ideas to trigger additional ideas. One member of the group should make a list of all of the ideas.

Brainwriting and Mind Mapping - Brain writing and Mind Mapping are two additional tools to generate ideas.

Brain writing

Brain writing is similar to free-association brainstorming, except that it is conducted in silence. This method encourages participants to pay closer attention to the ideas of others and piggyback on those ideas.

Before a brain writing session, create sheets of paper with a grid of nine squares on each sheet. You will need as many sheets as there are participants in the brain writing session with one or two extra sheets. Plan to sit participants in a circle or around a table. Determine how long the session will last, and remind participants that there is no talking. Remind participants of the other rules for brainstorming, especially deferring judgment.

For the session itself, state the problem or challenge to be solved. Each participant fills out three ideas on a brain writing grid. Then he or she places that brain writing sheet in the center of the table and selects a new sheet. Before writing additional ideas, the participant reads the three ideas at the top (generated by a different participant). The hope is that these items will suggest additional ideas to the participants. The participants should not write down the same ideas they have written on other sheets. This activity continues until all of the grids are full or the time runs out. At the end of the activity, there should be many ideas to consider and discuss.

Mind Mapping

Mind mapping is another method of generating ideas on paper, but can be conducted alone.

The problem solver starts by writing one main idea in the center of the paper. Write additional ideas around the sheet of paper, circling the idea and connecting the ideas with lines. This technique allows for representing non-linear relationships between ideas.

Duncker Diagrams

Duncker Diagrams are used with the present state and desired state statements discussed in chapter four. A Duncker diagram generates solutions by creating possible pathways from the present state to the desired state. However, the Duncker diagram also addresses an additional pathway of solving the problem by making it okay not to reach the desired state.

Duncker diagrams can help with refining the problem as well as generating ideas for solutions. The diagram begins with general solutions. Then it suggests functional solutions that give more specifics on what to do. The diagram can also include specific solutions of how to complete each item in the functional solutions.

For example, Michael wanted to address the problem of his job being too stressful. He is responsible for managing up to 1500 work hours per month. He cannot find a way to complete all of his tasks within a desired work week of no more than 45-50 hours per week. He has over 10 years' experience in public account and is interested in moving into industry. However, he is so busy, that he does not even have time to look for a new job.

The present state and desired state statements are:

- **Present State**: Job requires more demands on my time than I am willing to dedicate to a job I do not really care about.

- **Desired State**: Work a job I care about with adequate free time to spend with family and pursuing personal interests.

Here is what his Duncker diagram might look like.

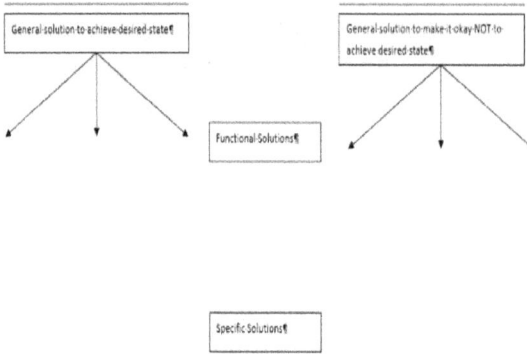

General solution to achieve desired state¶

General solution to make it okay NOT to achieve desired state¶

Functional Solutions¶

Specific Solutions¶

Case Study

Pamela and Lindi were arguing more than brainstorming, even though they had removed their mental blocks with regards to the problem at hand. They had spent two days trying to figure out the best approach to their problem, but hadn't achieved anything. Lindi suggested they use the Brain-writing method to deal with their problem, and invite others to join in. The following day, Pamela, Lindi and ten other co-workers, drew up grids on paper and submitted three ideas in absolute silence, using deferred judgment to do so. They swapped the papers and continued writing ideas for thirty minutes. At the end of the session, both Pamela and Lindi were overjoyed that the session had produced hundreds of solution suggestions to their problem.

The Morphological Matrix

Fritz Zwicky developed a method for general morphological analysis in the 1960s. The method has since been applied to many different fields. It is a method of listing examples of different attributes or issues to an item (or problem), and randomly combining the different examples to form a solution. Depending on the number of issues or attributes identified, there can be quite a large number of possible combinations.

The Morphological Matrix is a grid with several different columns. The problem solvers enter a specific attribute or issue about the item or problem at the top of each column. Then for each column, problem solvers generate a list of examples for that attribute. Once there are many different ideas in the columns, the solutions can be combined strategically or randomly. While some combinations naturally are incompatible, problem solvers should not rule out ideas until they reach the analysis phase of the problem-solving process.

For complex problems, computer-assisted morphological assessment can be done. However, for the scope of this course, we will look a simple example that can be done by hand.

As an example, let's look at the traffic problems experienced at a new elementary school. The administrative staff of the school has identified the problem statement as: "Get approximately 500 students to class safely, on time, and with no more than a five minute wait for parents and drivers in the neighborhood." A few sample attributes to this problem are safety, timeliness, pedestrians, and drivers.

A sample chart might look like this:

Safety	Timeliness	Pedestrians	Drivers
Extra cross guards	Stagger arrival time by grade	Cross only at crosswalks with crossing guard	Students being dropped off from cars or buses enter at north entrance
Policeman giving tickets for rule breakers	Provide incentives for dropping off early	Pedestrians enter at south entrance	Lane for drop off; lane for passing

This matrix can help identify different considerations of the problem. It can also help formulate comprehensive solutions to complex problems.

The Six Thinking Hats

Dr. Edward de Bono introduced a concept for thinking more effectively in groups in his book, *Six Thinking Hats*. The premise of this idea is that the brain thinks about things in a number of different ways.

The identified different categories of thought are assigned to a color-coded "hat," as described below. The hats provide a structured way to think about different aspects of a problem.

1. **White hat – Facts and Information**: This hat includes Information collected or identified as missing.

2. **Red Hat** – Feelings and Emotion: This hat includes feelings, including gut reactions to ideas or items identified in another area.

3. **Black Hat – Critical** Judgment: This hat includes details about obstacles to solving the problem or other negative connotations about an item or idea. Since people are naturally critical, it is important to limit black hat thinking to its appropriate role.

4. **Yellow Hat – Positive Judgment**: This hat is the opposite of the black hat. It includes details about the benefits of an idea or issue, or thoughts about favoring an idea. It is still critical thinking and judgment, as opposed to blind optimism.

5. **Green Hat – Alternatives and Learning**: This hat concerns ideas about new possibilities and thinking about implications rather than judgments. Green hat thinking covers the full spectrum of creativity.

6. **Blue Hat – The Big Picture**: This hat serves as the facilitator of the group thinking process. This hat can be used to set objectives both for the problem solving process and the thinking session itself.

The six thinking hat methodology allows a deliberate focusing during problem solving sessions, with an agreed-upon sequence and time limit to each hat. It ensures that everyone in the group is focused on a particular approach at the same time, rather than having one person reacting emotionally (red hat) while others are being objective (white hat) and still another is wearing the black hat to form critical judgments of ideas.

The green hat is the main thinking hat for generating solutions in the problem solving process. The other hats can be used as a reminder of the rules of productive brainstorming sessions, such as limiting critical judgment (positive and negative – yellow and black hats).

The Blink Method

Malcolm Gladwell popularizes scientific research about the power of the adaptive unconscious in his book *Blink: The Power of Thinking Without Thinking*. Gladwell's premise is that in an age of information overload, our decisions based on limited information are often as good as or better than decisions made with ample critical thinking.

In the examples and research Gladwell presents, experts and average subjects alike are better able and happier with choices made through what he calls "thin-slicing," or coming to a conclusion with limited information. An example presented is the case in which many experts identify a statue as a fake, when the museum that spent money on the statue did not identify it as such with weeks of research.

Gladwell also presents the cautions of the adaptive unconscious. Our power to make effective decisions by tapping into this power can be corrupted by personal likes and dislikes and stereotypes. Rapid, intuitive judgment can have disastrous consequences, as presented in his example of an innocent man shot on his own doorstep 41 times by New York policemen.

Gladwell summarizes the dilemma between when to tap into our unconscious, and when to use a more critical approach as thus: "On straightforward choices, deliberate analysis is best. When questions of analysis and personal choice start to get complicated – when we have to juggle many different variables – then our unconscious thought process may be superior."

Case Study

Judy and George were stuck late at work, figuring out how to organize an important corporate function which will take place the following Sunday. Their notes were scattered across the desk, and the room was in a state of disorganization until George suggested they use the Morphological Matrix to work out their problem. He asked Judy for her list of ideas on how they could stagger the arrivals, organize the eats and set out the schedule for the meeting and the speeches. Judy provided her ideas and George gave his own, and together they placed them in a table layout to create the best possible solution. George was relieved that they could contain their thoughts, use critical judgment and create a solution based on the table.

Chapter 7 – Analyzing Solutions

With many different solutions in hand, the problem solvers need to analyze those solutions to determine the effectiveness of each one. This chapter helps participants consider is the criteria or goals for solving the problem, as well as distinguishing between wants and needs. This chapter also introduces the cost/benefit analysis as a method of analyzing solutions.

Developing Criteria

Return to the information generated when defining the problem. Consider who, what, when, where, and how that the potential solution should meet to be an effective solution to the problem.

When developing criteria that possible solutions to the problem should meet, also consider the following:

- Ask questions such as "Wouldn't it be nice if..." or "Wouldn't it be terrible if..." to isolate the necessary outcome for the problem resolution.

- Think about what you want the solution to do or not do.

- Think about what values should be considered.

Use the answers to these questions as the starting point for your goals or problem-solving criteria.

Additionally, the criteria for an effective solution to the problem should consider the following:

- **Timing** – Is the problem urgent? What are the consequences for delaying action?

- **Trend** – What direction is the problem heading? Is the problem getting worse? Or does the problem have a low degree of concern when considering the future of the circumstances?

- **Impact** – Is the problem serious?

It is important to think about what the circumstances will look like after a successful solution has been implemented. Use your imagination to explore the possibilities for identifying goals or criteria related to the problem.

Analyzing Wants and Needs

The creative problem solving process is a fluid process, with some steps overlapping each other. Sometimes as the process provides additional information, problem solvers need to go back and refine the problem statement or gather additional information in order to effectively solve the problem.

Wants and needs seem like a fundamental aspect of defining the problem. However, in order to analyze the potential solutions, the wants and needs for the desired state after the problem is solved must be very clear.

Needs are items the potential solution absolutely must meet. If the potential solution does not meet a need requirement, you can disregard it from further analyzing.

Wants are nice to have items. You can provide a weight to each item to indicate its importance. For each potential solution, you can provide a rating for how well the solution addresses the selected want. Multiply the rating by the weight of the want to score the potential solution.

With scores for each item, it is an easy matter to rank the potential solutions in order of preference.

Using Cost/Benefit Analysis

Cost – benefit analysis is a method of assigning a monetary value to the potential benefits of a solution and weighing those against the costs of implementing that solution.

It is important to include ALL of the benefits and costs. This can be tricky, especially with intangible benefits (or costs). Some benefits or costs may be obvious, but others may take a little digging to uncover.

For example, imagine you want to replace three employees with a machine that makes stamps. A hidden benefit is that you may be able to use large feed stock instead of individual sheets, saving materials costs. In the same example, you would not only consider the salaries of the employees, but the total cost for those employees, including benefits and overhead.

The value assigned to the costs and benefits must be the same unit, which is why monetary value is suggested. The valuations assigned should represent what the involved parties would actually spend on the benefit or cost. For example, if people are always willing to save five minutes and spend an extra 50 cents on parking closer, they are demonstrating that time is worth more than 10 cents per minute. The considerations should also include the time value of money, or the value of money spent or earned now versus money spent or earned at some future point.

Case Study

Joseph, Kyle and Victor were spending the afternoon in the conference room, discussing the viability of their marketing solution for a new product. They were struggling along until Kyle suggests they use the Cost/Benefit Analysis to assess whether they're approaching the market in the correct way. Victor provided them with a few points which discuss the financial cost of the new strategy whilst Joseph pointed out the benefits. Together they analyzed the wants and needs of the clientele and analyze whether the product will fit the market, and how much it will cost them to implement the marketing strategy. In the end Kyle was happy that he suggested the technique and that the group banded together to analyze the marketing solution and figure out whether it was the best one available to them.

Developing Criteria Exercise

What is the timing of the problem?

What should be considered for the trend of the problem?

How serious is the problem?

Make a list of criteria the school district might consider for evaluating solutions.

1.

2.

3.

4.

5.

Cost-Benefit Analysis

Costs		Benefits	
	$		$
	$		$
	$		$
	$		$
	$		$

Chapter 8 – Selecting a Solution

The next step in the process is to select one or more solutions from the possibilities. In the previous step, you will have eliminated many of the possibilities. With a short list of possibilities, you can do a final analysis to come up with one or more of the best solutions to the problem. This chapter discusses that final analysis, as well as a tool for selecting a solution called Paired Comparison Analysis. It also discusses analyzing potential problems that may arise with a selected solution.

Doing a Final Analysis

In the previous stage of the process, you performed a cost/benefit analysis. However, since we cannot always know all of the potential variables, this analysis should not be the only one you perform.

For each potential solution, you must weigh the potential advantages and disadvantages. Consider the compatibility with your priorities and values. Consider how much risk the solution involves. Finally, consider the practicality of the solution. It may be helpful to create a map for each solution that addresses all of the relevant issues.

Consider the potential results of each solution, both the immediate results and the long-term possibilities.

In the final analysis, you will refine your shortlist and keep re-refining it until you determine the most effective solution.

Paired Comparison Analysis

The Paired Comparison Analysis tool is a method of prioritizing a small number of workable solutions. The first step for using this tool is to list all of the possible solutions. Label each potential solution with a letter or number.

Next, compare the solutions in pairs. Decide only between those two which solution is preferable. Assign a number to indicate the strength of the preference for each option. For example, problem solvers could assign a "3" to items they strongly prefer, a "2" to a moderate preference, or a "1" to a mild preference.

This first round continues two at a time until all of the solutions are ranked. Then all the ranks are added together to obtain a priority score for each item. The top score is the preferred solution.

For example, imagine that a group of children are deciding which fairy tale to perform in a school play. They have listed six favorites:

A) Sleeping Beauty   B) Cinderella
         C) Snow White

D) Jack and the Beanstalk   E) Hansel and Gretel
         F) The Three Little Pigs

Their chart might look like this:

A-B2   A-C3   A-D3   A-E1   A-F1

         B-C1   B-D2   B-E1   B-F2

                 C-D3   C-E1   C-F2

                         D-E2   D-F2

                                 E-F3

A = 1   B = 5   C = 4   D = 12   E = 1   F = 6

In this example, the clear winner is choice D, or Jack and the Beanstalk.

Analyzing Potential Problems

Think forward to the solution implementation. Ask how, when, who, what, and where in relation to implementing the solution. Does the imagined future state with this problem solution match the desired state developed earlier in the process?

Brainstorm for potential problems related to the solution. Consider how likely potential problems might occur and how serious they are. These potential issues can then be evaluated as needs and wants along with the other criteria for evaluating the solution.

Sometimes this analysis can uncover a potential hardship or opportunity that changes the criteria, problem definition, or other aspects of the problem solving process. Remember to be flexible and revisit the other stages of the process when necessary.

Case Study

Gregory and Henry were sitting at their desks across from each other, working over the solutions they'd come up with to prevent loss of cash flow in their small business. They were frustrated by their inability to choose the best solution until Henry suggested they use the Paired Comparison Analysis, which would enable them to set out their solutions in a chart and compare them in pairs. Gregory and Henry assigned preference values to the pairs and categorically worked out which solution they preferred and which would work best for their purposes. In the end, Henry was glad they'd worked together to discuss and layout their preferences, and that they'd found the best solution to save their business money, using a final analysis.

Final Analysis Exercise

SOLUTION BEING ANALYZED:

ADVANTAGES:

(1)

(2)

(3)

(4)

(5)

DISADVANTAGES

(1)

(2)

(3)

(4)

(5)

COMPATIBLE WITH SCHOOL DISTRICT PRIORITIES AND VALUES?

(1)

(2)

(3)

(4)

(5)

RISK?

(1)

(2)

(3)

(4)

(5)

PRACTICAL?

(1)

(2)

(3)

(4)

(5)

Chapter 9 – Planning Your Next Steps

Once you have selected one or more solutions to the problem, it is time to implement them. This chapter looks at identifying tasks and resources, and re-evaluating the solution and adapting as necessary.

Identifying Tasks

This part of the creative problem solving process is the time to think about the steps for making the solution become reality. What steps are necessary to put the solution into place?

Brainstorm with people involved with the problem to determine the specific steps necessary to make the solution become a reality. At this stage of the process, working with a smaller group may be more effective, unless you need approval from a large group. While making that list, identify any tasks that are critical to the timing of the solution implementation. Critical tasks are items that will delay the entire implementation schedule if they are not completed on time. Non-critical tasks are items that can be done as time and resources permit.

Identifying Resources

This part of the creative problem solving process is the time to think about the resources for making the solution become reality. What else is necessary to put the solution into place?

The types of resources that may be involved are listed below, along with some questions to think about to assign resources to the project of implementing the solution.

- **Time:** How will you schedule the project? When would you like the solution completed? How much time will each task identified take?

- **Personnel:** Who will complete each identified task?

- **Equipment:** Is there any special equipment required to implement the task? Does the equipment exist or need to be obtained?

- **Money**: How much will the solution cost? Where will the money come from?

- **Information:** Is any additional information required to implement the solution? Who will obtain it? How?

Implementing, Evaluating, and Adapting

Once you have determined the tasks and the resources necessary to implement the solution, take action! Now is the time to use your project management skills to keep the solution implementation on track.

As part of the implementation process, you will also continue to evaluate the solution(s). It is important to be flexible and adapt the solutions as necessary, based on the evaluation of the solution's effectiveness at solving the problem. You may need to make adjustments to the plan as new information about the solution comes to light.

Case Study

Jeremy and Stacy were holed up in a hot office on a summer afternoon, after just creating and analyzing a workable solution to their accounting problem. Though they had the solution, they were still unsure of how to proceed. Stacy suggested they use the method of Identifying Resources to better understand their options for proceeding on to the actionable phase of implementing the solution. Jeremy agreed and was more than happy to oblige, and they wrote down their resources: time, money, personnel, equipment and information. With this information, they were able to create an action plan, and move forward to implement the solution. Stacy was happy that they had the resources and could identify them with Jeremy's expertise.

Identifying Resources Exercise

When Identifying resources, ask the following questions.

- How much Time is needed to implement the solution? When does it need to be complete?

- Who will complete each task?

- Is there any special equipment required to implement the task? Does the equipment exist or need to be obtained?

- How much will the solution cost? Where will the money come from?

- Is any additional information required to implement the solution? Who will obtain it? How?

- What tasks are needed to implement the selected solution?

- What are the critical tasks?

- What are the non-critical tasks?

Chapter 10 – Recording Lessons Learned

Once you have solved the problem successfully, it is time to apply what you have learned to make solving future problems easier.

Planning the Follow-Up Meeting

Have a follow-up meeting after the solution has been implemented. Here are some things to consider when planning this meeting:

- Make sure you have a clear agenda for the meeting. The purpose of this meeting is to conduct a final evaluation of the problem, the selected solution, and the implementation project. Use the follow up meeting to find out if any of the team members still have frustrations about the problem or its solution. It is also time to celebrate successes and identify improvements, discussed in the next two topics.

- Make sure to invite all of the team members involved with the creative problem solving process and the solution implementation.

- Make sure to consider the meeting arrangements, such as refreshments and equipment needed.

- Invite the participants in plenty of time, to make sure that all key members can be present for the meeting. Make such each participant knows the purpose of the meeting so that all have the appropriate incentive to attend.

Celebrating Successes

After the problem has been solved, take the time to celebrate the things that went well in the problem solving process. Try to recognize each person for their contributions and accomplishments.

You can celebrate successes by recognizing the contributions of the team members in the follow-up meeting. Alternatively, you can have a party or other form of celebration. A good activity just needs to help the team celebrate a job well done in coming up with all the solutions, evaluating them, and finally implementing a solution effectively.

Identifying Improvements

There have probably been some bumps along the road in the creative problem solving process. Take the time to identify lessons learned and ways to make improvements so that the next problem solved will be even better.

Meeting with team members and stakeholders to identify improvements is a valuable exercise for several reasons.

- It ensures everyone is aware of the challenges encountered and what was done to resolve them.

- If something is learned from a mistake or failed endeavor, then the effort put into the task is not entirely wasted.

- Participants can apply these lessons to future problems and be more successful.

Case Study

Hillary, John and Clinton were happy they had successfully implemented and managed the solution to their marketing problem. However, they were struggling to come up with a method of recording that success and using it to define and refine future solutions to similar problems. They were frustrated that they had come up with a solution but still didn't know how to record it. Tensions were rising until John suggested the hold a follow-up meeting, and Hillary and Clinton helped lay out an agenda, arrange a relevant time for the meeting and invite all those who were involved in implementing the solution. Afterwards, they planned a celebration and were happy that they had come to an amicable solution to yet another challenge.

Additional Titles

The 90 Minute Guide series of books covers a variety of general business skills and are intended to be completed in 90 minutes or less. It is an effective way for building your skill set and can be used to acquire professional development units needed by project managers and other industries to maintain their certification. For the availability of titles please see

https://www.silvercitypublications.com/shop/.

No. 1 - Appreciative Inquiry

No. 2 - Assertiveness and Self Control

No. 3 - Attention Management

No. 4 - Body Language Basics

No. 5 - Business Acumen

No. 6 - Business and Etiquette

No. 7 - Change Management

No. 8 - Coaching and Mentoring

No. 9 - Communications Strategies

No. 10 - Conflict Resolution

No. 11 - Creative Problem Solving

No. 12 - Delivering Constructive Criticism

No. 13 - Developing Creativity

No. 14 - Developing Emotional Intelligence

No. 15 - Developing Interpersonal Skills

No. 16 - Developing Social Intelligence

No. 17 - Employee Motivation

No. 18 - Facilitation Skills

No. 19 - Goal Setting and Getting Things Done

No. 20 - Knowledge Management Fundamentals

No. 21 - Leadership and Influence

No. 22 - Lean Process and Six Sigma Basics

No. 23 - Managing Anger

No. 24 - Meeting Management

No. 25 - Negotiation Skills

No. 26 - Networking Inside a Company

No. 27 - Networking Outside a Company

No. 28 - Office Politics for Managers

No. 29 - Organizational Skills

No. 30 - Performance Management

No. 31 - Presentation Skills

No. 32 - Public Speaking

No. 33 - Servant Leadership

www.ingramcontent.com/pod-product-compliance
Lightning Source LLC
Chambersburg PA
CBHW071741020426
42331CB00008B/2126